Content

Hypochondria

Fear of disease

How to finally understand the fear of illness and get rid of it step by step

incl. the best exercises for immediate self-help

Maike Ahlers

What you can expect in this book

Anxiety is a very serious issue and especially the fear of illness is a real ordeal for many sufferers.

But fear is also a feeling that every human being carries within him or her, which is vital or essential for survival and is stronger or weaker in each person depending on their personality. Fear drives, inspires, mobilizes one's own forces, leads to success, but can also make you sick - so sick that life becomes hell. Hypochondria - as the fear of illness is specifically called - is a phenomenon of completely exaggerated fears that can push sufferers to their limits. Neverthe-less - even if some may not believe it - sufferers are not malingerers.

In my guidebook, you can expect an exciting insight into the topic of anxiety with all its accompanying symptoms, tips for improving the symptomatology as well as specific suggestions for immediate implementation - of course suitable for everyday life, I promise!

Based on studies, you will also gain insight into the anxiety problem in Germany.

You will get to know a young woman who had a panic fear of illness and struggled with her fear on a daily basis, only to find effective methods to make it bearable for her. Fortunately, over time she learned to live better with her fear. Today, thanks to professional help and her own will, she is a happy woman.

You can do this too, and of course equally if you are a man (or diverse)!

Anxiety in general

UNDERSTANDING FEAR

Snakes, spiders, confinement in an elevator or airplane, in a tube, at heights, illness, being alone, even peanut butter or buttons - all or most people are afraid of something.

Anxiety is a normal feeling and not pathological - actually.

Every person carries this feeling more or less within himself. Whether the everyday little fears develop into a pathological fear that requires treatment is strongly related to the personality. There are people who fear less, while others scream and wince at small things. Still others cannot leave the house and are no longer socially acceptable. These people need professional help. Actually, their lives could also be happy and relatively free of fear. But those who have pronounced fears no longer see their happiness. They cannot go through life carefree and cannot enjoy their existence. Fear becomes an ordeal.

If you already wake up with a racing heart and drenched in sweat and no longer dare to go to work because you fear that you will not be able to look colleagues in the eye, that you will not be able to talk to them, that you will not dare to say even one word in return, and that this will turn your day into torture, then the fear is pathological - in this case a social phobia is emerging - and a trusting conversation with a doctor should take place.

But many of those affected do not go to the doctor, either because they do not know they are ill or because they are ashamed. They also don't want to be pigeonholed as mentally ill. Some people doubt whether their fears are still within the bounds of normality or whether they need serious help and should have their fears treated.

If you are experiencing anxiety that is making life difficult for you, be sure to read on and/or make a consultation appointment with your doctor/psychiatrist ahead of time, because the sooner you get help, the better.

Some people are downright consumed by fear, unsettled and rob themselves of such precious life energy. Others go through life with a smile, brimming with self-confidence, beaming with happiness and contentment, not understanding in the least the worries of the anxious.

Dear readers, you are now wondering why this is so?

Everyone has had a childhood that was more or less formative for them. But a bad childhood says nothing about how anxious a person actually is. Many circumstances contribute to this, for example the environment and one's own living conditions (if I live in a high-rise building with an elevator and I have a so-called claustrophobia, every day can become a burden just to see the elevator, but it can also help me overcome my fear).

Without fear, our ancestors would not have survived. Fear warns and makes alert at the same time. It ensured our ancestors' existence, their survival. The saber-toothed tiger was a real threat, just like predatory cats, wolves, poisonous spiders and snakes.

If people are afraid of snakes, it is not imaginary, but evolutionary. Snakes had and still have a venom that can be deadly for us humans. These primal fears and phobias of people go back to times when it was necessary for survival to protect themselves from this real danger. If people at that time had no fear of dangerous animals, they would not have survived. So those who had no fear of natural forces or dangerous animals died. Fear was life-saving and became ingrained in people over generations. Thus, fears were passed on and inherited by the next generation. Anyone who suffers from a fear of cats today can be sure that the primal fear of the saber-toothed tiger is behind it.

However, fear not only has an evolutionary background, but also a protective function. A Portuguese-American neurologist, for example, described a patient who no longer seemed to feel any fear because of a calcification deep inside her brain. Her fear center was virtually chronically shut off, so she always appeared cheerful and accommodating. She let strangers hug her and chatted with everyone. This fearlessness has not only advantages - it can be exploited very quickly and become a problem.

Our body is prepared in a dangerous situation for a possible fight or flight, so a reaction of the body to fear is a normal process. When the heart races with fear and tension, the muscles are better supplied with blood and breathing is accelerated, so that the oxygen content in the blood then increases.

However, if the tension (for example, the tightening of the hands) and rapid breathing persist for a longer period of time, the body cannot distinguish whether there is actually danger or not, and a reaction develops in which it discharges - a panic attack is the result.

Genes also play a major role in anxiety and are significant for its development. The inheritance of anxious genes is estimated at about 30 to 40 percent. Anxiety disorders have been observed simultaneously more often in identical twins than in fraternal twins. If one family member has an anxiety disorder, it is more likely that children and later generations will also suffer from an anxiety disorder than in families that are psychologically unaffected.

Some patients with panic disorders have a gene in them that is mutated and thus altered in its activity. Scientists have found that this genetic alteration can trigger uncontrolled fear sensations. Mice that carry this gene also behave extremely overanxious.

If you recognize yourself and know that you are one of those people who are always anxious, constantly worrying and sensitive, you can also be a little happy (even if it is not really comforting), because these are the people who are not the most boring. They have exciting things to tell and more imagination. Famous personalities also suffered from anxiety disorders, let's mention Goethe, Brecht, Vivaldi and even Freud, the founder of psychoanalysis.

One form of anxiety disorder is panic disorder, which affects approximately four percent of people around the world during their lifetime. Panic attacks occur suddenly and for no apparent reason. They are characterized by rapid heartbeat, shortness of breath, choking sensation or shortness of breath. Patients are drenched in sweat and tremble all over their bodies or feel as if they are about to faint.

In principle, however, there is not just one trigger. Scientists think these fears often stem from trauma in early childhood. The loss of a parent, experiences with violence, sexual abuse, neglect or parents who abused alcohol can promote the development of panic disorders or the development of mental illnesses in general.

Fear, however, should also be seen as an opportunity, the chance to turn the current precarious situation into a fuller happier life.

Fear in particular

In Germany, almost 10 million (!) people are affected by an anxiety disorder, with women being diagnosed much more frequently than men.

WHAT ARE THE FEARS?

One type of anxiety disorder is phobia, another type is panic disorder.

Panic disorder, unlike phobia, does not relate to a specific object or situation.

People who suffer from phobias have an extremely exaggerated fear of objects or situations that are actually harmless to them. Thus, the fear is actually unfounded. Nevertheless, the fear of the people affected by it is unreasonably great and they want to avoid this situation, which is extremely stressful for them, at all costs.

There are a whole lot of phobias that people can suffer from that you probably didn't have the slightest idea about before, such as alektorophobia - the fear of chickens - or koumpounophobia - the fear of buttons. There is also the fear of holes - trypophobia. This sounds pretty far-fetched and is probably not some-thing many people go to clinics to be treated for.

The following fears are most common among Germans:

- Panic disorders
- generalized anxiety disorder
- social phobia
- Agoraphobia
- specific phobias

Panic disorders

Panic disorder includes repeated panic attacks that cause very strong physical symptoms in the affected person. An extremely strong feeling of anxiety occurs very suddenly. The symptoms that sufferers experience include racing heart, severe dizziness, shortness of breath, feeling faint, chest pain or increased sweating. Many symptoms can occur at the same time. People feel that their heart is beating up to their neck, and it feels as if it is stumbling, which in turn raises the fear that they are about to have a heart attack. In the chest, they feel a tightness or pressure, or worse, stabbing pain. The throat feels constricted, they have a lump in their throat and the feeling of shortness of breath due to faster breathing. Panic patients feel like they can't breathe because of this and hyperventilate (they breathe excessively fast and more). The body is thrown into such turmoil that many sufferers have a panic fear of going crazy or even dying in these moments.

Such a panic attack usually lasts about 20 to 30 minutes, peaking after about 10 minutes. Rarely, people report that the attack lasts longer than an hour. For some people, the spook is over after a single panic attack, but more common are repeated attacks. They can occur several times a day. This leads to the fact that the affected persons develop very great fear of the attacks, which leads to a so-called "fear of fear" and ends in a vicious circle.

Fifty to one hundred million people worldwide probably suffer from panic attacks. The word derives from Greek mythology, where there was the god Pan, half-man, half-goat, who stalked unsuspecting travelers in a Greek province during the midday heat. He scared these people so badly that they ran away in fear and panic, and Pan disappeared just as quickly as he had come.

(Source: Herbig, R.: Pan, the Greek Goat God. Attempt of a monography. Frankfurt, Vittorio Klostermann 1949)

Generalized anxiety disorder

A typical feature of generalized anxiety disorder is that people who are affected by it tend to worry about everything, constantly and over a long period of time. This does not mean their own worries and musings, but these people worry about their family, relatives, children, spouse or significant other. The worries concern many everyday areas of life and can always involve different issues. Some worry that something might happen to a close relative or friend, others worry about their professional future and about getting into financial trouble. Sufferers feel as if they are in a trance; they are plagued by dizziness, uncertainty, weakness, and lightheadedness, but also, as with panic disorder, have symptoms such as a racing heart, shortness of breath, chest pain, a lumpy feeling in the throat, nausea, dry mouth, and/or hot or cold shivers. These people cannot relax, they are constantly under stress, nervous and plagued by restlessness, they are in a state of constant tension. This in turn leads to tense muscles, which then eventually begin to ache.

People with generalized anxiety disorder do not have sudden anxiety attacks as in panic disorder, but are in a constant state of anxiety throughout the day. This is then not as intense, but lasts much longer. Most of the time, these people know about their exaggerated fears, but still cannot control them or can do so only with difficulty.

They also suffer permanently from sleep disturbances, they cannot fall asleep because they are stuck in a mental gyroscope and constantly have to think about their worries. Individual complaints can also occur again and again in different combinations.

Furthermore, generalized anxiety disorder is characterized by jumpiness and irritability, difficulty concentrating, tension headaches, and sometimes abdominal discomfort.

Often these physical symptoms are misinterpreted by the doctor and so begins an odyssey from doctor to doctor. On average, it takes seven years from the first symptoms to the correct diagnosis.

Overprotection in childhood as well as neglect by parents can lead to a person developing a generalized anxiety disorder in the course of his or her life. Hereditary factors also play a role that should not be forgotten.

Social phobia

Are you afraid of people? Are you afraid to be in their company, to communicate with them, to interact with them, to speak in front of others, to express yourself in company, to eat together with colleagues during lunch break or even to meet the opposite sex? Do you feel hand tremors, nausea, stomach discomfort, do you blush or do you have to go to the bathroom all the time? Are you afraid of being criticized, embarrassed, judged negatively or even humiliated? Do you constantly avoid eye contact? Are you terribly afraid of exams so that you can't even take them?
Then it could be that you suffer from social phobia.

Unlike shyness, people with social phobia completely avoid situations in which they are exposed to human contact. Their fear of talking to or making contact with strangers is so great that they may only be able to get through this while taking medication. In the process, people with social anxiety experience a significant reduction in their quality of life.

Social anxiety is evident at an early age, usually during puberty.

If children have already gone through experiences in kindergarten or elementary school that were socially stressful for them, if they were laughed at, rejected or constantly teased by others, this can lead to inferiority, insecurity and great anxiety in these children. Usually, such stressed children then no longer dare to say anything at all at school, because they always have the feeling that what they are saying is wrong.

Children who experience violence in the family, whose parents live in divorce, who receive little love or where there is a mentally ill parent, have an additional increased risk of developing social phobia. Parents who teach their children that they are in the way, constantly disrupting them and not welcome, may develop low self-esteem. On the other hand, children of overprotective parents do not learn how to deal with mistakes. For all parents with children, please refer to the following song: "Everyone makes mistakes, no one is a superman" by Rolf Zuckowski. Listen to this song, move to it with your children and thus strengthen your child's self-esteem!

Agoraphobia

Agoraphobia is triggered by certain places and situations. Those affected experience a panic fear of public places or crowds of people. Some are afraid to go to a shopping market for fear of not being able to breathe there. Others cannot go into the woods because they are obsessed with the thought that a sudden event might happen, such as suffering a heart attack, and then there is no one in the woods to help them. These fears cause people with agoraphobia to develop marked avoidance behaviors to avoid these fear-inducing situations.

Typical are also fears like sitting crowded in a crowded streetcar, in a bus or in a train or even flying in an airplane. There, in case of a panic attack, there is sensation and no escape - they think. If no countermeasures are taken in this regard and the anxious person does not end their avoidance, it develops into a fear of fear and this in turn leads to a restriction of their activities and general limitations in their daily life.

According to statistics, about four out of every one hundred people develop agoraphobia in the course of a year, with more women affected than men. Around the age of 30, on average, agoraphobia appears for the first time.

The cause may be an altered balance of certain neurotransmitters in the brain, but a hereditary pre-disposition is also possible.

It is not uncommon for people with agoraphobia to remain anxiety-free for a long period of time. If they avoid the situations or places that scare them and therefore have no trigger for their fear, they can live completely carefree for a long period of time. However, as soon as they take control again and go "into the woods" again, the panic fear is back.

The recommended therapy here is cognitive be-havioral therapy.

Specific phobias

Imagine going to the zoo, standing in the terrarium and marveling at all the animals that wriggle there and that you can make out between the wooden beams - larger and a little smaller animals, but all without legs and with a strong muscular body. They see them lambent and crawling very slowly down the small trunk. Some are lying on the branch or coiled around it, others are wriggling along the ground.

Does that scare you? Like Nadine, who was persuaded to try visiting the terrarium again after all? Nadine walks into the zoo building overcautiously, always holding her hands in front of her face, putting one very small step in front of the next and always ready to escape. Today she wants to be brave, very brave. Today she will prove to her husband what a tough, fearless woman she is. Today is the day she dares a confrontation and resolves not to look away and not to run away in the first place. No, today she doesn't want to run away, today she is brave.

The snakes are all behind glass, nothing can happen, yes, her husband is good to talk. It is not the fear that something could happen, it is pure disgust with Nadine. She already can't stand the sight of such a drawn animal, even as a small child she couldn't look at the picture book where the hedgehog bit the snake. Or was it the other way around? Nadine would never trouble her memory again, because although she still kept that pencil sketched children's book in her closet, she never looked at it again. She always wanted to get rid of it, but she just can't touch it. Today, however, is the day Nadine wants to gather all her courage and go into the terrarium she so dreads. Her husband tried to talk her out of all her fear in advance, Nadine was very skeptical, but after all she is a woman in her late thirties, already in the middle of life and professionally recognized and even very popular. However, she preferred to leave her little Paul with grandma and grandpa today to spare him her possible screaming. Long story short: Nadine has very courageously approached, piece by piece, actually millimeter by millimeter to the glass front surface of the first terrarium and still sees: nothing... Suddenly Nadine goes through a fright, which could not be bigger, then a scream, an insanely loud scream, and Nadine runs loudly roaring out of the building and immediately her extremely panic fear is back.

Her heart races, her pulse beats up to her chest, she shakes with disgust. Nadine suffers from an extreme snake phobia. She wanted to manage to overcome her terrible fear this time, and although she knows that the animals can't harm her, she hasn't managed to keep her fear in check.

Cognitive behavioral therapy or confrontation therapy can help here. If you are affected as badly as Nadine, do not be afraid to contact a psychologist. There are, of course, other specific phobias, such as fear of heights, of flying in an airplane, or of natural forces, such as water. These feared situations are then avoided by those affected, even though they know that their fear is exaggerated and that there is usually no danger involved.

HYPOCHONDRIA - UNFOUNDED FEAR OF ILLNESS

Charlie Chaplin had it, Frederick the Great, Woody Allen and Thomas Mann were also affected - about one percent of Germans have it, the unfounded fear of illness. These people have a great fear of illnesses that they don't actually have. They misinterpret their symptoms, spend hours on the Internet researching every little sign of their body, imagine they are seriously ill, and are the most thoroughly examined patients at their doctor's office. They constantly need the doctor's reassurance, and even when the doctor certifies that everything is fine, the thought of the doctor's credibility doesn't last too long. Then the insecurity becomes so great and they think that they are very sick after all and just no one has determined it yet. This then leads to what is called "doctor hopping." Hypochondriacs run from doctor to doctor, hoping that someone will find something so that they feel confirmed in their belief.

On the other hand, they are also afraid of their own diagnosis being confirmed. Because they constantly observe and control their own bodies and are so fixated on themselves, every little thing is reinterpreted or misinterpreted, such as a headache into a brain tumor or abdominal discomfort into colon cancer. This was the case with Theo, who had made many visits to his family doctor, with many referrals to specialists. Everything was examined, the lungs, the heart and the liver, he was to the gastroscopy, intestinal endoscopy and bladder endoscopy, to the CT of the entire abdomen (abdominal cavity), additionally to the MRT, he was to the nephrologist, internist, surgeon, cardiologist and pneumologist - but none of these doctors could confirm his bad assumption of the intestinal cancer. Meanwhile, he was suffering from massive abdominal discomfort and it could only be cancer. Theo was actually ashamed of his many visits to the doctor, but he was so convinced that he was terminally ill that he couldn't help it.

Theo was not a malingerer, he did not imagine his symptoms and faked them, no, he really felt the pain and discomfort every day. He had developed a hypochondriacal delusion that restricted him greatly and affected his quality of life enormously. He used to go to soccer games with friends, but now he spends hours researching his alleged illness in front of a computer. As a result, friends have withdrawn. In order to find a way out of his isolation and the vicious circle, his family doctor has now advised him to undergo psychotherapy. Theo is determined to take advantage of it and make his life worth living again without this constant psychological burden.

Around forty percent of those affected also suffer from depression at the same time. Theo was also increasingly plagued by insomnia, had no drive and his mood became increasingly depressed. This was due to his childhood. As a child he was seriously ill and his mother was overprotective. She dramatized his illness even more, so that Theo learned that his whole life was marked by terrible illness.

Individual therapy with a psychotherapist is not the only way to conquer hypochondria; group therapy can also be helpful. For patients with depression, it may also be appropriate to administer additional antidepressants. Biofeedback may also be helpful. Through the screen, patients are made aware that symptoms can be normal and harmless. Patients should internalize this as much as possible.

CORONA - THE FEAR OF A VIRUS

Since 2019, when the coronavirus broke out in China and in March/April 2020 also increasingly frightened Germany, the fear and panic could no longer be ignored by many people. The news rolled over, every week there were new restrictions, then in the individual states again a few relaxations and many people were distraught about all that was still unclear.

We humans need a certain amount of security, and insecurity causes fear. This could be seen, for example, in the enormous hamster purchases. The population was suddenly overcome by panic, a completely new situation arose for many and they thought that the spread of the coronavirus could lead to shortages in the food supply. Some people felt such uncertainty and got irrational fears. And panic can be contagious....

Additionally, the Corona issue had (or has) such a large presence in all media, with constant disaster reports and bold headlines driving up the spiral of fear, which in turn led to a feeling of being helplessly at the mercy of this invisible virus and powerless against it.

In these times, it is important for people not to be unsettled by these many reports and not to consume the negative news permanently. Of course, you should inform yourself, but if you are already very anxious by nature, you should not subject yourself to this scaremongering even more. In such life situations, rather pay new attention to your free time by using the more available time more consciously and intensively, for example, to discover new hobbies, you start reading again or try to consciously perceive nature once again with all its scents and smells. Listen to your favorite music, dance to it and steer your thoughts away from anxiety and panic. Sports are also a good way to reduce stress. Now you don't have to become a competitive athlete, walking and/or strolling will also suffice. You can do this alone or with your partner and maybe in the best case it will even enrich your partnership! There are also free online courses and virtual sports on YouTube that can be accessed at any time. Also, be aware of what positive things you can take away from this time, something that will enrich your life. Maybe take it upon yourself to become more grateful, grateful that you live in a country with a high standard of health, or be

· grateful for your children and family, grateful for every single day you get to enjoy!

MANY SYMPTOMS - ONE POSSIBLE CAUSE: FEAR OF ILLNESS

If you feel the symptoms you have already read about and secretly know that you are suffering from an anxiety disorder, do not be afraid to see a doctor. Go once more rather than too little and do not be ashamed of it. Many other people feel the same way you do.

Here are some more warning signs or symptoms that might show up if you have a fear of illness:

very great fear of suffering from an incurable disease; worry about pain; fear of having to sit in a wheelchair or of becoming disabled in general; exaggerated perception of body signals; insecurity; constant visits to the doctor and reassurance; panic attacks; fear of having to suffer badly and no one can help; in extreme cases, fear of death.

This can also manifest itself in palpitations, dizziness, loss of concentration, hot flashes (can also occur during menopause), exhaustion and constant fatigue, as the body's reserves of strength are depleted by the constant tension. Fear of illness also often affects the gastrointestinal tract and manifests itself in increased diarrhea, stomach or abdominal discomfort, and constipation, sometimes alternating with diarrhea.

Many affected persons perceive their bodies very carefully, for example, they constantly examine their breasts, inform themselves very intensively about possible signs of disease and then see the descriptions as applicable to them.

However, the following is very important: Affected persons are not malingerers! They really feel the symptoms.

Research results

Getting cancer is the most feared disease for the German population. No other fear of disease haunts the minds of the local people more. In general, although most are quite satisfied with their health, i.e., more than half of those surveyed in a study rate their state of health as good, and a third even rate it as very good, 10 percent still see their condition as poor or very poor (2 percent). In contrast to older people, those under 45 rate their health status as "rather good" or "very good" (Forsa study 2019). Nevertheless, for many, the thought of getting cancer is an idea they would prefer to quickly banish from their minds.

Since 2010 - every November - surveys on Germans' fear of illness have been conducted by the renowned Forsa Institute for the health insurance company DAK-Gesundheit.

The current 2019 study looked like this with 2814 survey respondents:

Cancer remains the most feared disease among the German population, regardless of the age of the respondents. Fear of tumors thus topped the list of all feared illnesses at 69 percent. One in three people is afraid of mental illnesses, i.e., depression, burnout and anxiety disorders - this applies to all age groups and has remained the same since the analysis began in 2010.

The 69 percent who are afraid of developing a malignant tumor are followed by 49 percent who are afraid of dementia or Alzheimer's disease, 45 percent are afraid of strokes and 43 percent of respondents are afraid of serious accidents and injuries in the process. Fear of a heart attack was cited by 38 percent and 33 percent would never want to get a serious eye disease, including blindness. Women are more fearful of this than men, with the exception of heart attacks. Older people fear strokes and Alzheimer's disease as well as dementia more than younger people.

A serious lung disease is something 21 percent do

not want to get, diabetes 16 percent and 11 percent fear a venereal disease.

Furthermore, the study states that there are differences in the individual federal states. According to the study, most people feel fit in Schleswig-Holstein (a full 95 percent), followed by Baden-Württemberg and Bavaria (both 90 percent). According to the study, people in three German states are not quite as satisfied with their health: Saxony-Anhalt (80), Saxony (83) and Thuringia (85).

In Saarland, the fear of cancer is particularly widespread, as indicated by 79 percent of respondents. In Hesse, on the other hand, most fear Alzheimer's (55) and serious accidents (58).

Women are more health- and duty-conscious than men, they attend cancer screenings more often (69 percent) and are more open to stress management exercises. Of the men, only 45 percent reported going for preventive care.

Here is an overview once again:
These 10 diseases are the most feared:

- Cancer (69 %)
- Alzheimer's disease/dementia (49 %)
- Stroke (45 %)

- Accident with injuries (43 %)
- Heart attack (38 %)
- Severe eye disease (33%)
- Mental illness (30 %)
- Severe lung disease (21%)
- Diabetes (16 %)
- STDs such as AIDS (11%)

(Source: Forsa survey 2019 commissioned by DAK)

The R+V Insurance Info Center also deals with studies and has been investigating the "Fears of the Germans" every summer for almost 30 years.

For a current occasion, there is a study from the beginning of April 2020 on the Corona fear in Germany, which the Info Center of R+V Insurance has conducted and thus prompted a special survey with 1075 citizens.

The following four questions were asked of the participants:

1.   Do the high infection rates increase the fear of severe disease?

2.   Do more people fear a recession now? (economic downturn)

3.   How great is the fear of losing one's job?

4.   How do Germans rate the work of politicians?

Here, we will specifically address only the first question, which can be answered unequivocally in the affirmative.

By six percentage points, the fear of becoming seriously ill increased to 41 percent overall during the Corona crisis. There is no notable difference in age groups. Previously in the course of the study, the younger generation up to the age of 30 was significantly more carefree than their elders. Now, apparently, many young people have also understood that Covid-19 can affect them, too.

Fear of serious illness is again significantly higher among women in this special survey (46 percent) than among men, only 36 percent of whom reported this.

Sarah's struggle with fear

Sarah is a young woman of 36 years, tall, pretty to look at with long blond, slightly wavy hair. She lived in a steady partnership for ten years until her boyfriend broke up with her three years ago. Sarah was in a deep crisis at that time, she was so focused on herself that actually a man had no place in her life. Sarah's boyfriend loved her, but increasingly he could no longer cope with the situation, which was extremely difficult for him. He missed the affection, their deep love, which was still there at the beginning of the relationship, he missed the togetherness, the cuddling and the sexual passion. There were conversations, but Sarah blocked, retreating more and more into her inner self. She already loved him, but she couldn't get out of her skin, she couldn't get involved with anyone else at this point - Sarah only saw herself. She paid attention to every little sign of her actually so attractive body. She noticed every little change in herself. For hours she stood in front of the mirror, not to look at her beauty, no, she bit herself into a state, of which she had never believed to experience it once. Sarah was sick - very sick...

Meanwhile, everything started so harmlessly...Sarah grew up as an only child in her parents' house; her father was an engineer in a large company, her mother was an executive secretary at an energy provider. She received the full attention of her parents, who had little time but a lot of love for their daughter. Strictly speaking, this meant that her father gave Sarah a lot of physical attention in the form of affectionate hugs, while Sarah's mother showed her love more through abundant culinary supplies; she cooked, sizzled and baked with devotion.

The mother was also mentally unstable, very anxious, sick from time to time, she was the stricter of the two, but still she loved her daughter in her own way. So Sarah experienced from her mother less loving honest hugs, little caresses and cordiality. She unconsciously always felt her mother's timidity. Her mother did not want vacations to other countries where one could only get by plane, she worried excessively when Sarah came home a little late, she unconsciously transferred her own fears to her daughter. Sarah didn't notice any of this at first. The parents separated when Sarah turned 18. Thus she experienced a childhood that was characterized on the one hand by the honest love of her father, but on the other hand by an unconsciously experienced coolness of her fearful mother.

Sarah's boyfriend could visibly handle it worse, he saw how Sarah suffered more and more, withdrew, no longer paid attention to him. He still loved her, but he could no longer live with Sarah's behavior, so the separation was inevitable for him. In this crisis, Sarah fell into such a deep hole that she only found her way back to a happier life with professional help.

But how did Sarah's condition manifest itself?

THE DEVIL IN HER

Sarah stood in front of the mirror every morning. First for 10 minutes, then for half an hour, later for 2 hours. Her body was trembling, her heart was racing, her pulse was beating so fast that she was scared again and again. "I'm about to have a heart attack, I'm going to fall down, nobody helps me, nobody is there, I'm all alone here, I'm going to die...". In these moments, so terrible for her, Sarah had only these terrible thoughts. It was so threatening for her that she screamed in such moments. Sarah had no more strength, her body reared up, her pulse raced even faster, to infinity...Sarah's body rebelled. She kept having panic attacks that right now everything will be over, that she will die, now really. Panic attacks crept up again and again. For Sarah, it was quite a terrifying experience. Once experienced, the fear now circled around not to experience this again. A vicious circle began.

Once again, Sarah grabbed the phone in her panic and dialed 911. Each time, she shook all over, shouted frantically that she was having a heart attack, that she was dying, that she couldn't breathe, and then the cell phone usually fell out of her hand... Minutes later, the emergency doctor arrived, took an EKG of her heart, measured her pulse, and took her to the hospital as a precaution. Sarah was sure each time that it had to be very bad now - after all, otherwise the ambulance would not have raced to the hospital with blue lights. In the emergency room, after all the necessary examinations had been carried out, a very level-headed and thoughtful doctor explained to her this time that there was nothing wrong with her physically, but that she had gotten so carried away that the symptoms actually felt like a heart attack, but that she could rest assured that everything was fine with her heart. This calmed Sarah down for the moment and when she was discharged again, she could believe the doctor for a short time, but when she stood in front of the mirror again a few days later in the morning, fate took its course once again.

Sarah couldn't help looking at herself in the mirror, taking a close look at her body, and so days later Sarah stood in front of her mirror again, looking at herself from all sides, and then she discovered it - a mole she had never seen before. She immediately started researching on the Internet what a "normal" mole should look like. Oh no, this brown little spot was uneven and somewhat frayed, at least that's how it appeared to her, oh that can't be - skin cancer, yes I have skin cancer! Again, a devil began to spread inside Sarah, a devil that was taking her mind away. Her heart began to beat faster, she became short of breath, dizziness set in, another panic attack was brewing. Everything was spinning in her head. "I do have something wrong with my heart, and I also have skin cancer". The mental carousel wouldn't stop, the dizziness wouldn't stop, Sarah dialed 911....

That was three years ago now.

ACCEPTANCE

This time, a young assistant doctor made the same statement as the last times, that Sarah's heart was healthy, and that she should see a dermatologist to have the mole examined to be on the safe side. That same day, Sarah called the dermatologist and got an appointment that same week due to her expressed panic, which caused renewed panic to erupt in her mind. "If it's that fast of an appointment, then the mole must be especially dangerous!". Sarah's mind went even more crazy and now she was constantly in front of the mirror during the day as well, looking at herself even more closely. She was constantly looking at the mole, even getting a magnifying glass. Sarah's anxiety increased immeasurably each time. Heart palpitations, dizziness and an alternation of hot and cold shivers spread.

"I have skin cancer, skin cancer, skin cancer, yes it must be, otherwise I would have had an appointment in a quarter of a year!". The three days until her appointment with the dermatologist were hell for Sarah. Sarah could no longer concentrate on her work as a freelance artist. Meanwhile, she had so much to prepare for the next exhibition at the museum... "But what's the point of it all, with skin cancer my life will be over soon anyway...". The fear in Sarah's head grew and grew and grew...and didn't leave her a quiet minute anymore. Sarah trembled constantly, could not sleep at all the last nights until the appointment, at night she rolled from one side to the other, her thoughts circled around the mole that was so bad for her, around her entire life, around her relationship, was it even still one (?), she was sweaty in the morning and drenched in sweat in the evening....

The doctor, who was calmly looking at her mole and examining it closely with a magnifying glass, spoke very soothingly and kindly to Sarah, who was almost hysterically talking to the doctor, but he remained very calm, shook his head and was actually able to curb Sarah's terrible fear a little. The mole didn't look alarming, it was a normal little spot that didn't seem alarming at the moment and would only need medical attention if it really changed.

But what the reassuring doctor still said to Sarah initially seemed completely strange to her: she should discuss it with her family doctor and, if necessary, present herself to a psychologist. With a psychologist? Sarah didn't believe it...

A few days later, Sarah internalized the doctor's words. For the first time, she really realized for herself that something was wrong with her, and after much thought and research on the Internet, she knew and understood: she is sick. She is a hypochondriac, her panic fear exceeds the scope of normal many times over. No, she did not imagine her dizziness, even the pulse beating up to her neck was real, yet she accepted what she had not done before: she accepted herself with all her suffering and accepted the doctor's words.

YOUR WAY BACK TO NORMALITY

Sarah summoned up all her courage and made an appointment with her family doctor. Her excitement was boundless, her hands sweaty and cold in turns, her forehead felt hot, she was shaking all over when she entered the practice. She was so excited that she forgot her name. In the waiting room, her excitement increased even more, but when Sarah realized that she was here to get help, she was able to calm down at least a little bit. This reassurance then increased more and more through the trusting conversation with the doctor.

First of all, it should be mentioned that it is also possible to consult a psychiatric specialist. The family doctor can also issue a referral to this.

Of course, Sarah hardly dared to speak out her problem at first, but since she noticed that the doctor was looking at her in a friendly way and smiling slightly, and since she knew inwardly that her life could not go on like this, Sarah overcame her shame, mustered all her courage and, in tears, told the doctor: "I am very afraid of illness! At that moment, a stone fell from Sarah's heart, she trembled, but no panic attack followed. Immediately seeing the seriousness behind Sarah's statements, the doctor made her aware in a kindly decisive way that she was not alone with her problem, that she did not have to be ashamed of it and that there was help for Sarah. Her doctor's words left a trace of hope and Sarah increasingly understood that it was now up to her to follow this path that had been pointed out to her and to contact a psychological psychotherapist for cognitive behavioral therapy. At the same time, her doctor did not conceal the fact that there are long waiting times for appointments, and she advised her to immediately request a list of therapists from the health insurance company and to contact various therapists. Each therapist has what are called probationary sessions, where the patient and therapist get to know each other and decide if a therapeutic relationship is possible for them. Furthermore, these sessions, of which there are a minimum of two and a maximum of four since 2017, clarify which therapy seems most suitable and, of course, a detailed diagnosis also takes place.

Sarah's doctor made her very aware that she would have to see her doctor urgently if she were so unwell that she could no longer structure her day, fell into deep depression or even thought of suicide. In that case, admission to a psychiatric hospital would be urgent and represents immediate help. With all these words and pointed out possibilities of her doctor and still holding a referral to a psychotherapist in her hand, Sarah left the practice. At first, all that was said overwhelmed her a bit, but Sarah was now insightful enough to follow her doctor's words, get everything going, and even three weeks later she had an appointment with a psychotherapist for a preliminary consultation.

After two sessions, it was clear to Sarah that the chemistry between her and the therapist was right, that she could open up to him, and that she was ready to answer all of his comprehensive questions about her life situation, specifics of her personal development, including educational and professional development, in order to lay the groundwork for successful therapy.

Sarah felt better and better after each therapy session and understood more and more that her fear of illness had its roots in childhood. With the help of the therapist, she worked through her relationship with her mother in particular in a cognitive behavioral therapy session and dissolved old behavioral patterns. This gave Sarah a new perspective and gradually freed her from her terrible fears. She even learned to trust her mirror again. She could accept herself, look in the mirror early, briefly examine the mole, notice that it had not changed, not make a big fuss about it and look forward to her day.

Life can be so beautiful after all.

Increasingly freed from her fear of serious illnesses, Sarah is also ready again for a new love, for a partner who accepts her as she is, with whom she can become happy. Her newfound self-confidence encourages her in this. Sarah has also discovered a new hobby for herself, completely free of charge and very effective, as she herself has discovered more and more: walking in the beautiful countryside. She does this at least three times a week, has scheduled fixed days for it, and no longer has to force herself to do it. She feels a real longing for it, because she has noticed that her head is much freer after walking, she feels good and it has a very positive effect on the quality of her sleep. The musings have become much less, she no longer tosses and turns for hours in bed, which in turn gives her freshness and balance for the next day - what a nice side effect, and so the vicious circle is broken!

Of course, there are days when Sarah's thoughts wander and she gets stuck on old times, but Sarah has

learned and internalized therapy approaches that
allow her to turn her thoughts away and change them
for the better. You'll find out exactly how in a moment.

Exercises for immediate implementation

Every crisis in your life or here especially also the powerless feeling of excessive fear carries incredible chances. Recognize your problems and use them as a turnaround in your life! Face your fear! Say stop to your current state and use the following possibilities to get out of your fear:

Medical help / psychotherapy or cognitive behavioral therapy

Go to a doctor! You can go to your family doctor or psychiatrist/psychotherapist and address your fears there. The sooner, the better! By doing so, you can prevent anxiety from manifesting itself in your life. After all, you want to live a happy life and not let fears define you! In any case, seek medical help and be ready for therapy! You can choose between individual and group therapies, and the doctor will advise you. Anxieties are also easily treatable. In the case of phobias, for example, confrontation therapy could be applied, that is, those who have a phobia of spiders will be cured most quickly if they let the creepy-crawlies run over their arm. This may sound absurd at first, but it is crowned with success, even if you cannot imagine it at the moment and it makes you shiver. At first, this imagination of a spider on your arm could also be done only mentally, in that you endure this occurrence mentally and only then come to the real situation. In detail, the therapist will find the best way with you! Recognize your fear and stand by it and yourself! We humans tend to always want to "make everything go away" or "have it go away" quickly, but if we realize that our fear is simply a part of us and belongs to our personality, if we learn to accept it, then it will not dominate us so much anymore.

Acceptance of your fear

Do not judge yourself and your feeling of fear! Accept WHAT IS!

You have created the feeling of fear in your life once yourself. When the fear arises in you, perceive it consciously, accept it as a loving feeling, say YES to yourself, say YES to your fear:

"YES you, my fear, you may be with me now, you are a part of me at the moment, I don't send you away, I accept you! I have created you and accept you as my feeling".

Close your eyes and feel your fear acutely when it tries to work its mischief in you once again. It will rise up inside you and try to dominate your body, but it will also pass away if you simply accept and embrace it like a friend. Acceptance means love and love is the key to a fulfilled happy existence and life.

Self-acceptance is the best thing you can do for yourself, because after all, you are the most important person in your life! So take good care of your feelings of fear, be radically honest with yourself and your fear will become less if you allow it and adopt a loving attitude towards it. In this way, the feeling of fear can be transformed, because every bad feeling only arises when it is negatively judged.

Medication or combination with behavioral therapy

If you need medication to help with your anxiety, please also check with your doctor.

There are so-called selective serotonin reuptake inhibitors (SSRIs), which are used for many psychiatric disorders. Serotonin is found in our nervous system and is also called the "happiness hormone". It is a so-called neurotransmitter that influences various processes in the body, including our emotions, the central reward system, and also our mood and drive. Therefore, the administration of additional psychotropic drugs can be useful, since serotonin deficiency is associated with depressed mood and anxiety.

If you don't like taking medications, let me tell you, they are available not only as chemotherapeutic agents, but likewise as herbal alternatives, for example, in the form of high-dose St. John's wort.

However, since there are no studies on whether the effect lasts after the end of therapy, you should discuss the possibility of taking medication very carefully with your doctor and still consider it for the current acute case or for stabilization, or use it as a supplement to behavioral therapy.

Sports / outdoor exercise - the healing power of walks

You don't have to become a fast jogger, you don't have to run a marathon, but exercise in the fresh air is a good way to clear your head and simply feel good. Exercise releases happy hormones, also prevents many physical ailments, lets us relieve stress, release endorphins, which in turn lead to feelings of happiness, and reduce anxiety. Your well-being will thank you!

Start with short walks, daily if possible, even in cold and wet weather. This will also increase your immune system and make you feel healthier overall. You can also relieve inner tension, aggression and frustration. You will also strengthen your self-esteem and be less prone to depression and anxiety. Motivate yourself: "I can do this today". Take a friend with you for a walk, the motivation is even higher in pairs.

Also check with your health insurance company! There are many different sports courses that are offered and subsidized by health insurance companies. You can also meet like-minded people there. Choose a sport that you can enjoy and that you develop a sense of pleasure in. For people whose element is not water, swimming or kite surfing is not right either. Those who hate jogging may like hiking. You will find the right thing for yourself if you try it.

Qigong is an example for beginners. In this Chinese form of concentration and movement, which is also equivalent to meditation, body energies are activated and can flow better. Qigong serves for relaxation and at the same time leads to a better body feeling, has a regulating effect on the entire nervous system, refines self-perception and positively influences the emotions and our entire mood. Please feel free to inform yourself about it!

Maybe it will help you to resolve not to use the car every day in the future, but to activate the bicycle once again, starting with small routes, maybe just for small purchases. You will love it when it becomes a ritual.

Gratitude

Gratitude is a great tool for a fulfilled and happy life. In doing so, you don't have to say or think up any big gratitude phrases. Be grateful for your existence today! Every day is a gift, make yourself aware that it is a very big gift that you are allowed to be in the world, that you live in peace, that you have enough to eat. Every night before you go to sleep, say to yourself three sentences: "I have been grateful today for...".

The best thing is to internalize your gratitude and let it become a fixed ritual and part of your day or evening by acquiring a small gratitude booklet and formulating three sentences a day about what you were grateful for today. These don't have to be big things or complicated ways of thinking, just enjoying a butterfly is enough. "I am grateful that I saw this beautiful butterfly today". Or consciously enjoy your cup of tea, focus on the taste and say, "I am grateful for this enjoyable tea." If you do this every day, your life will change in a positive way. It won't happen overnight, so keep at it and do it!

No catastrophe thinking!

Stay in the here and now! Look at what is really there in the moment. Notice sounds and smells consciously, concentrate on what you are doing or seeing right now! Banish your negative thoughts about yesterday, tomorrow or the day after tomorrow, stay with today and in the present moment. Don't think about what was negative yesterday, what bad things could happen tomorrow and what catastrophe is heading your way the day after tomorrow. You can do this by immediately saying stop to yourself, stop thinking the thought and look around at what is surrounding you right now. Immediately realize that it is only thoughts that are running through your head right now, and don't believe all your thoughts.

Say to yourself, "It's just a thought." You can still question your thought: "Is my thought really true?", "Can I really be sure that this thought is true?".

With this, you quickly come to a clear statement. You do not know namely whether your thought or also your catastrophe thinking will really become true. Therefore you stop the negative thought immediately!

Direct your attention to your breath!

Make yourself comfortable, this can be an armchair, the couch, a cozy lounger or a nice spot in the garden, on the park bench or wherever you feel comfortable. Feel your breath!

Consciously breathe in slowly, hold your breath for a moment, and just as consciously breathe out again slowly. Repeat this exercise several times. You may do well with the so-called 4-7-8 method, which you can use when you feel a panic attack coming on or the anxiety is very high.

In this breathing technique, you inhale slowly for 4 seconds, hold your breath for 7 seconds, and exhale for 8 seconds. The exhale can be quietly noisy. This will regulate blood pressure and calm your nervous system. Repeat this exercise about 4 times. If you use this exercise daily, you can immediately get your body under control and calm down when anxiety rises.

However, you can also try a different counting method:

Count from 1 to 10 as you inhale, then count to 5 as you pause to breathe, and count backwards from 10 to 1 as you exhale. Couple this exercise with an image in your mind: think, for example, of a butterfly that sits down on a bush, remains seated, and then flies away again. Or the sea and the waves as they slowly crash onto the beach and then disappear into the sea again. There are no limits to your imagination here.

Self-love and self-confidence

Take time for yourself and do something good for yourself every day. Ask yourself the question, "What do I need today to feel good and have a good day?" because you are the most important person in your life.

Accept yourself with all your weaknesses and faults, because these are human and belong to you. You are valuable and right as a human being even when you are anxious. You too deserve a good life!

Believe in yourself and your energy and be kind to yourself. Decide what you allow others to do and where your boundaries are.

Stop whining and complaining! Life has new challenges for each of us every day, it holds dangers every day, but also many new opportunities. Try to recognize them and welcome them as something positive. Also pay attention to a positive environment and do not surround yourself with negative people.

Define positive thoughts, for example, "I am good the way I am" or "I deserve happiness."

Think about the future. What do you still want to achieve in your life? Do you want to continue your current career as it is or is it time for a change? Be brave to allow thoughts of change. Maybe you have never been really happy in your job, in your relationship, etc.? Don't shy away from your thoughts, but embrace them and try to figure out what you want your life to look like in the next few years.

Clearly formulate your plans and goals!

Positively clarify the meaning of your life.

Allow yourself time alone as well! Make sure you take time out in your everyday life and allow yourself breaks and beautiful moments. Enjoy the sight of meadows, trees, streams, flowers, mountains and water consciously alone. Smell the flowers along the way and be mindful of the many beautiful little things and moments.

Relaxation techniques

Learn relaxation techniques such as Progressive Muscle Relaxation according to Jacobsen, known as PMR for short, or autogenic training. You will experience a physical and mental state of relaxation that leads to a reduction in emotional tension. Your health insurance company can tell you about courses for this. You can also ask at sports studios, and even physiotherapists offer courses. It is also possible to apply for psycho-somatic rehabilitation. You are welcome to ask your pension provider about this.

Forest bathing

Against anxiety and tension also an excellent remedy is forest bathing.

Draw your strength from nature and use nature for your well-being and against your fears. During forest bathing or conscious walks in the forest you are very close to nature, you can breathe freely and feel unobserved. You can listen to the birds, observe small insects and smell the moss. The peace and harmony of the forest reduces stress hormones and the greenery of the plants has a calming effect on the nerves. In the forest you can completely find yourself, you can become a child again. Look for small flowers, weave a wreath, blow into blades of grass, creating sounds, just like when you were a child! Jump, hop, be happy consciously, but also take breaks in the forest again, again and again, feel the clear air, open your senses and just perceive! Be mindful! Walk barefoot once and feel the unevenness, the different materials on the ground or the warmth or coolness of the moss, the roots.... Feel yourself!

Conclusion

We humans all have fear. Some of us have a fear of actual danger, that is, a fear that keeps them alive and protects them, and some others have an unfounded fear that is not useful and is pathological, blocking them and upsetting them and their lives.

In every fear and in every fear of illness in particular, there is also an opportunity. To recognize this chance means to find out what you do not see in your life so far, what you do not want to admit. Every fear honestly shows us our condition, has a deep meaning and at the same time a task. This is what we have to recognize. The sick and anxious person is not an innocent victim, but also a perpetrator himself. His symptoms of fear of illness show themselves physically, but they are psychological conflicts which must be unmasked as problems of the person.

The question arises: how can you be healthy if you suffer from anxiety that makes your day difficult, that makes it impossible for you to live a carefree life at the moment?

It is essential in this case to seek professional help in the form of psychotherapy or behavioral therapy and not to focus on all the little symptoms that seem to dwell in the body like ghosts, but to live in the here and now, to notice the beauty of nature, to receive the love of the family and to feel a great gratitude every day and to be consciously mindful. It is hard and difficult, but it is worth it to find yourself. It is a process of duration and it does not happen overnight, but keep at it, for your own health, for your own happiness in life, for contentment and well-being.

When you have a problem, you want to get rid of it as quickly as possible. But it doesn't work quite that simply in life. Everything takes time. This, in turn, is worth investing. It is an investment for you! Even if it is a lengthy process to recognize that you have an anxiety disorder, it is extremely useful to deal with yourself and your life and your history of anxiety in order to emerge from the problem strengthened and full of life to go your further way.

So: Face your fear! Learn relaxation techniques and mindfulness! No one has to be ashamed of their anxiety. Seek professional help in the form of psychotherapy and get rid of old prejudices that psychotherapy is a method of treating the mentally disturbed. For more and more people, psychotherapy for anxiety disorders is a very helpful tool and one of the best methods to experience consciousness, to get to know yourself better and to understand yourself with all your behaviors, thus paving the way for more self-confidence and self-love. You should not overstretch your expectations, but it is worth it in any case, even if the road is hard and rocky.

You will conquer your fear!

You are worth it to live a fear-free and carefree life!

You can do it!

All the love!

www.ingramcontent.com/pod-product-compliance
Lightning Source LLC
Chambersburg PA
CBHW051315160726
47994CB00003B/1461